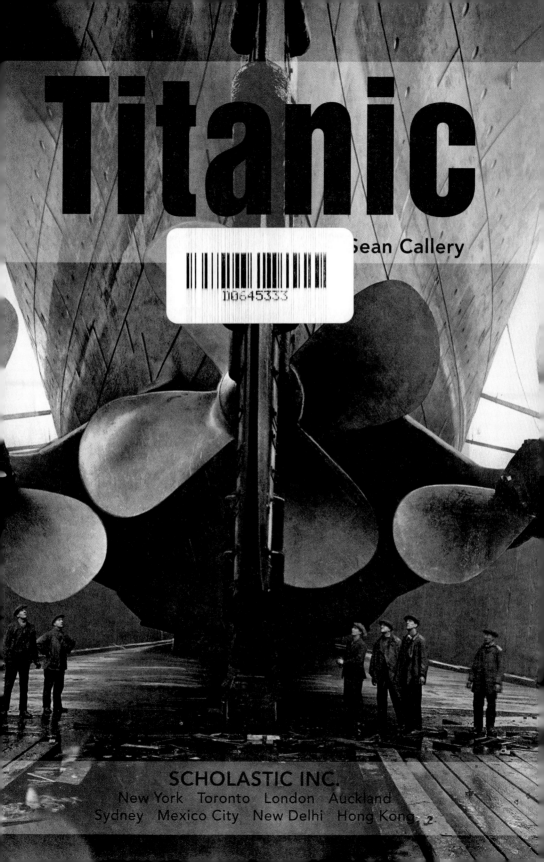

Titanic

Sean Callery

I0645333

SCHOLASTIC INC.

New York Toronto London Auckland
Sydney Mexico City New Delhi Hong Kong

Read more! Do more!

After you read this book, download your free all-new digital activities.

For Mac and PC

Take fun quizzes about the facts in this book.

Play games and activities with videos and sounds!

Log on to
www.scholastic.com/discovermore/readers
Enter this special code: **L3C2RPRHJFK3**

Contents

EDUCATIONAL BOARD: Monique Datta, EdD, Asst. Professor, Rossier School of Education, USC; Karyn Saxon, PhD, Elementary Curriculum Coordinator, Wayland, MA; Francie Alexander, Chief Academic Officer, Scholastic Inc.

Titanic sinks!

Titanic tilted down into the water. All its lights went out. Terrified people clung to the sides of the ship. With a huge noise, *Titanic* split in two and sank. The screams of 1,500 people filled the freezing air. Far away, survivors in lifeboats held hands as they watched and listened in horror. One of them was Eva Hart. She knew that her father was in the icy water.

Young eyewitness
Eva Hart, age seven, sailed on *Titanic* with her parents. Later, she wrote about what she had seen.

SOS

Eva Hart saw the ship

> I have lived and relived the dying moments of the *Titanic* many times since I sat cold and miserable, crying for my father, in that small lifeboat bobbing about on the icy waters of the Atlantic.

2,223 passengers and crew members

This was the scene in the early morning of Monday, April 15, 1912. *Titanic*, the ship that everyone said was unsinkable, had hit an iceberg. It filled with water and sank within hours. *Titanic* is the most famous shipwreck in history.

The ultimate ship

Titanic was the world's latest wonder. It was the biggest, most luxurious ship on the seas. *Titanic* was built in Belfast, Ireland, by a team of 15,000 men. Inside, it looked like a palace. First-class passengers could eat at fancy cafés or swim in the pool. Second-class bedrooms were very comfortable. Third class had a big room for music and dancing. Most homes did not have electricity, but *Titanic* was lit by 10,000 lightbulbs.

1 captain, Edward John Smith

898 crew members

This is the hull of *Titanic*'s sister ship. *Titanic* was slightly bigger.

Titanic by the numbers

About 3 million rivets held the ship together.

Titanic had 1,200 portholes.

The ship was 11 stories tall and 882.8 feet (269 m) long.

NEW WORD

Very rich people often live in **luxurious** (luhg-ZHOOR-ee-uhs) homes.

SAY IT OUT LOUD

The most expensive ticket cost about $87,000 in today's money.

To feed the passengers and crew, *Titanic* carried:

40,000 eggs

1,000 loaves of bread

36,000 apples

Titanic was as luxurious as a nice hotel. It also had the latest safety features. People thought that it was unsinkable. It had special areas that were supposed to be watertight. Even if the ship was damaged, it would stay afloat. People could be rowed to safety in lifeboats.

The lifeboats were stored on the top deck. They were lowered on ropes from steel arms.

THINK ABOUT IT **If you were on board**

Titanic was ready to sail from England to the United States on April 10, 1912. The world was watching the "ship of dreams."

Radio

Titanic had the latest radio equipment. This could be used to call for help if needed.

Radio headset

Each red area was watertight...

Watertight sections

The hull, or bottom frame, was split into 16 watertight areas.

Lots of lifeboats

Titanic had more lifeboats than the laws called for. The 20 lifeboats could carry 1,178 people. This was half of the people on board.

Titanic, would you think the ship was safe?

On board *Titanic*

All kinds of people sailed on *Titanic*. The very rich traveled in first class. Among them was Margaret Brown, an American returning from a vacation in Europe. Passengers in second class might be teachers or businessmen, like

Southampton, England

The wreck

New York, US

Atlantic Ocean

Titanic's route

Titanic was set to sail more than 3,000 miles (4,800 km) across the ocean.

SOS

Between 1901 and 1910, 8.8 million

First class:
Margaret Brown

Second class:
The Hart family

Third class:
The Goodwin family

Eva Hart's father. The Goodwins and their children were traveling in third class. Like many third-class passengers, they were leaving Europe to find a better life in the United States.

Everybody had heard about this . . . new liner being constructed for the White Star Line, and my father told us all about the comfort we could expect and what a good ship it was.

Eva Hart saw the ship go down.

This violin belonged to the leader of *Titanic's* band.

people traveled to the US seeking a better life.

The passengers explored *Titanic*'s many rooms. These fit like puzzle pieces around big spaces such as the grand staircase, the dining rooms, and the swimming pool. The chart room was at the top of the ship. Inside, officers figured out where the ship was and how far it had traveled.

In the depths of the ship, stokers sweated all day and all night, shoveling coal into boilers.

Titanic cross section

Chart room

Pool

THINK ABOUT IT **Why were third-class**

Grand staircase

First-class deck

B Deck: First-class café

F Deck: Third-class dining room

Boilers

cabins on the lower decks?

Life on *Titanic* was thrilling for every class of passenger. There was something for everyone in the family. Frederic and Daisy Spedden were traveling in first class with their son, Douglas, age six. Maybe their day looked something like this.

Frederic swam in the pool. He joined his family for breakfast. Then he and Douglas played with a spinning top on the first-class deck.

Children were allowed in the gym between 1 PM and 3 PM. Douglas rode the bicycle and the electric camel. Then he played

First-class passengers could use *Titanic*'s gym.

Titanic had a kennel for passengers' dogs.

with the dogs on board when the staff brought them out from their kennels.

The family took an evening promenade before Douglas went to bed. Frederic played cards until lights-out.

Passengers took promenades before dinner.

Iceberg right ahead

Icebergs are mountains of ice that float in the sea. They did not often float into the route that *Titanic* was following. But there was ice on Sunday, April 14. Nearby ships sent ice warnings to *Titanic*. Some ships stopped because of the danger, but Captain Smith sailed on into the night at high speed. He was sure that his lookouts would spot any trouble and that *Titanic* was a safe ship.

But it's hard to pick out an iceberg in a dark, calm sea. When one appeared just ahead, *Titanic* swerved but could not avoid it. The iceberg scraped along the side of the ship. Five watertight areas started to flood.

TIME LINE APRIL 14, 1912

April 14, 9:12 AM
Titanic received the first of many ice warnings.

April 14, 10:00 AM
Lifeboat practice was canceled. No one knows why.

April 14, 7:00 PM
Titanic sailed at its fastest speed so far.

April 14, 10:00 PM
New lookouts went on duty. Their binoculars were lost.

April 14, 11:07 PM
The last warning wasn't passed on to Captain Smith.

April 14, 11:40 PM
A lookout rang a bell and yelled, "Iceberg right ahead."

April 14, 11:40 PM
Titanic scraped against the iceberg.

Titanic bounced along the side of the iceberg at 11:40 PM. The noise alarmed some people. Many others kept sleeping at first. Eva Hart's family hurried to the boat deck, where the lifeboats were. Passengers put on life jackets. They were loaded into lifeboats, women and children first. Down below, the crew was fighting a losing battle.

The iceberg made gashes in *Titanic*'s hull. The watertight areas weren't sealed at the top. The crew tried to keep water from flowing out of them and filling up the ship.

April 14, 11:40 PM
The iceberg badly damaged *Titanic*'s hull.

April 14, 11:41 PM
The engines went silent. *Titanic* began to drift.

April 14, 11:55 PM
Mail clerks found that their storage room had flooded.

April 15, 12:05 AM
Captain Smith told the crew to get the lifeboats ready.

April 15, 12:15 PM
The band started playing music, to help keep passengers calm.

April 15, 12:25 AM
Thomas Andrews, the ship's designer, knew *Titanic* would sink in two hours.

April 15, 12:25 AM
Titanic radioed for help from any nearby ships: "We have collision with iceberg. Sinking."

Benjamin Hart put his wife and daughter into Lifeboat 14. He watched as it was lowered. But a lot of people felt safer on the ship and would not climb into the lifeboats. Many were launched only half full. Then it became clear that there were not enough lifeboat seats for everyone

SOS

The last two canvas lifeboats were

on *Titanic*. At least one officer fired his gun in the air to keep men from storming onto one of the lifeboats. As *Titanic* filled with water, the crew struggled to launch the four canvas-sided lifeboats, like the one in this picture.

Titanic life jacket
Life jackets had cork inside them, to keep wearers afloat.

Eva Hart saw the ship go down

[My father] said: 'They are going to launch the boats. Purely a precaution; you will all be back on board for breakfast.'

washed into the sea as *Titanic* sank.

The last moments

Horrified survivors watched from the lifeboats as *Titanic*'s rows of glowing lights inched toward the water. Then the sea flowed over the front of the ship. *Titanic* broke in two. Its bow sank right away. The stern rose up in the air, with people clinging to decks that had become walls. Then it sank, dropping people into the freezing sea. Survivors heard their screams for help, then silence.

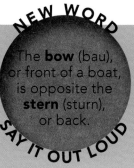

NEW WORD

SAY IT OUT LOUD

The **bow** (bau), or front of a boat, is opposite the **stern** (sturn), or back.

Should we stay away?

The people in the lifeboats argued. Should they go back for those in the water? Some were afraid that they would all drown if too many people climbed in.

Titanic splits

Titanic split in two, and its bow fell away.

Should we return?

Others felt that they should try to save lives. Officer Harold Lowe moved people to make room. He rowed a lifeboat back and pulled four people from the sea.

Floating stern

The stern floated for a minute. It rose up. Then it plunged to the seabed.

Carpathia picked up all of *Titanic's* survivors.

Most of *Titanic's* lifeboats were stored on *Carpathia*.

Carpathia, another ship, was 58 miles (93 km) from *Titanic*. It dodged icebergs through the night and found *Titanic's* lifeboats and their freezing passengers. Many survivors had lost everything except the clothes on their backs. *Carpathia's* passengers gave what they could.

Carpathia's passengers helped the survivors and gave them clothing to keep them warm.

Survivors' names were radioed ahead to New York.

A large crowd greeted the survivors when they landed.

Most of the survivors were women and children. They looked on *Carpathia* for husbands, sons, and brothers. Eva Hart had been parted from her mother when people were moved between lifeboats. She was alone when she was put in a large bag and lifted onto *Carpathia*. Eva knew her father was lost, but she found her mother.

Eva Hart saw the ship go down.

" I started screaming for [my mother]. . . . It was not until we had all been picked up that we found each other, many hours later. "

25

Sea robot

Jason is a deep-sea robot that was used to find *Titanic*.

Discovered!

For 73 years, no one knew where *Titanic* lay. Then, in 1985, a US-French expedition sent a robot down into the ocean and found the stern on the seabed. This showed that *Titanic* had broken in two before sinking. The bow was found 1,970 feet (600 m) away. More expeditions

Sonar image

This computer-made image shows *Titanic*'s bow on the seabed.

THINK ABOUT IT **Is it right or wrong to**

Bottles of wine

Luggage

A bathtub

explored the famous wreck. Thousands of items were taken from the seabed.

Finding *Titanic* sparked interest in the tale of its sinking. Many books and movies have told the stories of the heroes and villains on the "ship of dreams." They ask: Could things have been different?

Titanic's propeller blades sit on the seabed...

NEW WORD

An **expedition** (ek-spuh-DISH-uhn) can take you on a journey to somewhere new.

SAY IT OUT LOUD

take objects from *Titanic*'s wreck?

What do you think?

Here are some of the things that went wrong for *Titanic*. Could they have been different? Read your book again. What do you think?

High speed

Titanic sailed toward an ice field at high speed, ignoring radio warnings.

Watertight areas

The tops were not sealed. If one overflowed, the next one flooded.

Lost binoculars

The lookouts could not see very far. Their binoculars were missing.

Bad decision

Captain Smith did not change course to avoid the ice field.

Not enough lifeboats

There were no lifeboats on the first-class deck, because they spoiled the sea view.

No practice

A lifeboat drill was canceled. The crew had not practiced lowering all the lifeboats. They struggled to do it quickly.

Wasted space

Many lifeboats left with empty seats. Most did not return for survivors.

Californian

Another ship, *Californian*, was only about 17 miles (27 km) away. It did not come to help.

Distress signals

Its captain ignored *Titanic*'s distress rockets. He thought they were just greetings.

Glossary

binoculars
A tool that makes faraway things look larger and clearer.

boiler
A device that heats water and produces steam to provide power to something.

bow
The front of a boat or ship.

café
A small restaurant.

canvas
A type of coarse, strong cloth.

cling
To hold on to something very tightly.

collision
A sudden striking together of two things.

distress
Danger, or the state of needing help.

drift
To be moved by water or wind, not by a person or an engine.

electricity
A kind of power that travels through wires.

engine
A machine that makes something move.

expedition
A long trip made for a specific reason, such as for exploration.

eyewitness
Someone who saw something happen and can describe it.

gash
A long, deep cut or hole.

hull
The frame or body of a boat or ship.

iceberg
A large piece of ice floating in the sea.

kennel
A place where pets can stay while their owners are away.

launch
To set a boat or ship afloat in water.

lifeboat
A small, strong boat carried on a larger boat and used in emergencies.

life jacket
A vest that keeps a person afloat.

Titanic **sank in 2 hours and 40 minutes.**

lights-out
A signal that it is time to turn out the lights and go to sleep.

liner
A large, luxurious ship.

lookout
Someone who keeps watch for danger or trouble.

luxurious
Grand, comfortable, and expensive.

plunge
To fall heavily or sink quickly.

porthole
A small, round window in a boat or ship.

precaution
Something done in advance to keep something dangerous from happening.

promenade
A relaxing walk.

propeller
A set of rotating blades that moves something through air or water.

radio
A device that sends and receives messages, or to send a message using a radio.

rivet
A bolt that holds pieces of metal together.

seabed
The floor of the sea.

shipwreck
The destruction or remains of a ship at sea.

sister ship
A ship that is exactly or almost exactly the same as another ship.

sonar
A method of finding things underwater by using sound waves.

SOS
A distress signal, used by a ship or a plane that needs help.

stern
The back of a boat or ship.

stoker
Someone who keeps a boiler supplied with fuel.

survivor
Someone who lives through a disaster.

swerve
To turn suddenly, to avoid hitting something.

villain
A person who is blamed for something bad that happens.

watertight
Completely sealed so that water cannot get in or out.

Index